Speak the Word Over Your Family for Salvation

by

Harry and Cheryl Salem

06 05 04 03 10 9 8 7 6 5 4 3 2 1

Speak the Word Over Your Family for Salvation
ISBN 1-890370-17-7

P.O. Box 701287
Tulsa, Oklahoma 74170

Dedication

To our parents and families, through their example of household salvation and dedication they have shown us the importance of family, salvation, and relationship with God. Through good times and bad, they've remained steadfast in their commitment and strength, which comes from God.

List the names of the people you'll be praying for on this page.

Introduction

A few years ago the Lord spoke to our hearts and challenged us to begin to pray His Word out loud each day. I thought I was already doing that, but I quickly learned that I was only partially doing what He wanted me to do. God told us to activate His Word by praying it over our loved ones and friends each day.

The Lord said to me, "You think you have been praying My Word, but you have only been reading and saying My Word to me! I want you to write My Word out so that you can insert everyone's name into My Word, then I want you to go down the list of all the people you are to pray for each day and individually pray, not just say the words but pray with each person's name inserted right into My Word! Pray every word, My Word, out loud to Me. I will watch over it and perform it concerning the people whose names are inserted into each prayer. You activate My Word by praying it into the atmosphere."

We immediately began to dig through the Word, write out the scriptures, and allow the Holy Spirit to show us how to pray more effectively. After we wrote out just a few prayers, the Lord spoke to us again. This time He said, "Now that you know how to pray My Word, I want you to search My Word for effective scriptures to pray each day."

As we searched the Word we began to realize the vital importance of speaking God's words and not our own. Jeremiah 1:12 says, "Then said the Lord to me, You have seen well, for I am alert and active, watching over my Word to perform it."

Through this scripture we began to realize that God's Word activates the angels to accomplish God's will in our lives on this earth! That's why God *spoke* the world into existence, as an example to us, His children, of how to be creative and have God's kind of creative power and force upon this earth.

In Isaiah 44:26, "[The Lord] who confirms the word of His servant and performs the counsel of His messengers..." we quickly saw that God listens to what we say and then, because He set up the "power of the creative tongue" in Genesis chapter 1, He performs through His messengers—our words. That's why our words need to be His Words!

Isaiah 55:11 further establishes the importance of speaking and praying, "So shall My Word be that goes forth out of My mouth: it shall not return to Me void [without producing any effect, useless], but it shall accomplish that which I please and purpose, and it shall prosper in the thing for which I sent it."

We believe the most powerful scripture on speaking the Word of God out of our mouths when we pray is Psalm 107:20, "He sends forth His Word and heals them and rescues them from the pit and destruction." You might say, "Well, of course, when God sends His Word it works, but it's me doing the sending." NO!!!! You aren't doing the sending. You don't have any power to make words travel through time and space and affect a person's life. But God not only has this power, He uses us to speak His Word out of our mouths and then through the supernatural ways of God, these words transcend all realms: the natural realm, the emotional and mental (soulish) realm, and the supernatural realm. These three realms are all reality! God's Word moves into all realms the minute it comes out of our mouths and begins to "self-fulfill."

Isaiah 61:11 says, "For as [surely as] the earth brings forth its shoots, and as a garden causes what is sown in it to spring forth, so [surely] the

Lord God will cause rightness and justice and praise to spring forth before all the nations [through the self-fulfilling power of His Word]."

What a powerful scripture! God's Word has a built-in, self-fulfilling power. It must do what it says it will do. When we say it out of our mouths concerning ourselves or anyone else, the Word must self-fulfill. Get the revelation of this powerful action when you pray and know that the minute you say it out of your mouth it is a done deal. It's done!

You might be thinking, *But what about a person's free will to choose for himself?* That's a very good question, and we have heard it many times since the Lord had us start to teach this way of praying. We asked the Lord about it.

You know, the Father God always has the answer to all of our questions even before we ask them! The Lord began to direct us to some of the scriptures that you are about to learn to pray over your family and loved ones.

Acts 26:18 is one of the first ones that God showed us to pray over our lost loved ones. It says, "To open their eyes that they may turn from darkness to light and from the power of Satan to God, so that they may thus receive forgiveness and release from their sins and a place and portion among those who are consecrated and purified by faith in Me."

As we began to pray our loved ones' names into this scripture, we soon realized the key here is that we are *calling* them. When you call someone on the telephone they answer! When you call your dog he comes. When you call your children to come in for dinner they come!

There is a great spiritual power in *calling* them! Then notice we are calling them *out of darkness into light!* It's very important to notice that those loved ones have been making decisions in the past based upon being in the dark. When you call them out of darkness into the light of God and then they make decisions, their decisions are not based upon the darkness in which they have been living. You have called them *out* of darkness and *into* God's light and now they can make decisions based upon the light that they came into *when you called them*!

Let's look at another scripture we have been praying that will help prove this issue. Look at 1 Peter 2:9, "But you are a chosen race, a royal priesthood, a dedicated nation, [God's] own purchased, special people, that you may set forth the wonderful deeds and display the virtues and perfections of Him Who called you out of darkness into His marvelous light."

Once again there is the "calling out of darkness" action. By inserting the person's name that you are praying for, you are literally calling them by name out of darkness and giving them the opportunity to come into the light and make decisions for the future based upon the light and not the darkness!

As you go on through the scriptures that are outlined in the next few pages, remember to speak them out loud. I recommend you do it morning and night. Don't ever do it while the ones you are praying for are listening. It's not their hearing you that makes a difference. It's your being obedient to speak God's Word out of your mouth concerning them and then God performing what you have spoken!

Morning and night is significant because the Bible says in Revelation 12:10, "...for the accuser of our brethren, he who keeps bringing before our God charges against them day and night...." If Satan stands and accuses day and night, then I feel it is important to speak God's Word as we pray day and night to counteract the accuser's words!

We were ministering in a church when this revelation of how to pray for our loved ones was fresh in our thinking. We were just beginning to grasp the full weight of what God was calling us to do and to teach. We shared the concept in one of the services and challenged the people to stop *just* praying, "Oh, God, save so and so and such and such..." which yielded no results. We challenged them to write out the names of their loved ones, family members, friends, and co-workers that they had been praying for and begin to speak the Word over them day and night.

When we returned to this same church eight months later, a woman who had been in our previous meeting came up to us with a big smile on her face and a wonderful testimony to share with us. She began to tell us how, in the meeting eight months prior, she had written several names in her Bible of close loved ones that she had prayed for but had seen no results. She opened her Bible and showed how in only eight months she had already crossed off four of the names!

She said, "I did just what you said. I quit begging God, and worrying God, and I started speaking God's Word over them." Within only a few weeks, her brother and sister-in-law, whom she had been praying for and witnessing to for years with no positive response, called her and asked how to get to her church.

She told them that she would come by and pick them up. They came to church and because they were in the light and not in the darkness, when the altar call was given, they both gave their lives to Jesus! Hallelujah! Did she supersede their will by speaking the Word of God over them? No, but she did give them an opportunity to make choices for their lives and their futures based upon being in the light instead of making decisions while still in darkness!

She went on to tell how her father who lived in another state would not respond to her witnessing, so she simply spoke the Word of God over him and believed God to "watch over His Word to perform it." Not much time passed and her father, who was a widower, met a lady he really liked. This lady was saved and went to church, so to be with her, he went to church. They began to get close, and to make a beautiful love story short, he got saved and completely gave his life to Jesus!

What's so interesting to us about this story is that the daughter had absolutely nothing in the natural to do with her father finding Jesus. She did not have to take him to church. She did not do anything, *except* speak the Word of God over her daddy and sit back and watch God fulfill His Word!

The stories of receiving Jesus are always to be continued, because with God, *life* is the key word and life goes on and on!

As we began to share this more and more with people, Harry had what I call a "mini-vision." He said the Holy Ghost impressed this upon his heart. Whatever you want to call it, Harry got the point. The Holy Spirit showed Harry how one day he would be in heaven and God would say to him, "Well done, My son." Then, as he went on into heaven he would meet his earthly dad who went home to be with Jesus in 1968.

He said his earthly daddy started telling him how proud he was of him for getting all these people saved and healed and filled with the Holy Ghost. His dad was so proud of how his son had a godly marriage and family, and how his grandchildren loved Jesus so much. Harry said about this time in the impression (vision) he was feeling pretty good about himself. Then his earthly daddy turned to him and said, "But where is my brother? Where is my sister? Where is my family? You knew them by name, you knew where they lived, you knew their addresses and their phone numbers. Why didn't you get them to heaven?"

Harry and I began to understand that this is our opportunity to lay aside any differences that we might have with any and all family members and begin to speak God's Word over them. All of a sudden earthly values didn't seem to hold any value. All that really matters is that all of our loved ones have an opportunity to receive the greatest gift of all—JESUS!

We began to speak the Word of God over any and all of his family and mine, too. If we weren't sure of their relationship with Jesus, we spoke the Word over them. Even if we were speaking the Word over some who already knew Jesus, that would be all right because everyone benefits from the Word of God getting on them!

Several months passed before we had an opportunity to go to some of these loved ones and spend time with them, but God made a way. For many of them it had been thirty years since there had been any contact. But God doesn't forget anyone. He wants everyone saved, healed, and filled with His Spirit.

We led many of them to Jesus when we saw them. We planted many seeds of love and acceptance into the others. *Everything is a seed* and it all produces a harvest. Above all, there was restoration of a thirty-year separation. The beauty of it all is that those precious loved ones planted wonderful seeds back into our lives. That was an immediate harvest! We are not the Savior; we just do our part and speak the Word of God and are available if God chooses to use us to do anything else!

We encourage you to stay strong. Don't let Satan get you discouraged. Being discouraged really means you have taken your eyes off of your Savior and have put your eyes back on the problem and circumstance. Remember, Romans

4:17 says, "Calling those things that be not as though they were...." Don't talk about your loved ones as if they will always be the way they are now. NO!!! Talk about them as if they are already walking in the full light of God. Talk to them as if they are and *treat* them as if they are! You will be amazed at what God will do when you *honor* His Word. The word honor in the Hebrew language means "to open the door." So open the door of God's Word into all your loved ones' lives by speaking God's Word over their lives. The Word works when your work the Word!

When Jesus called Simon, *Peter*, Simon was anything but *God's rock!* But Jesus was "calling those things that be not as though they were." If it's good enough for Jesus to practice "calling," I believe we ought to do it, too, and get Jesus kind of results!

On the next pages you will find many scriptures already written out so you can just insert your loved ones' names and speak the Word out of your mouth morning and night. Do it, and watch God do His thing!

Remember to pray in your prayer language after you have spoken God's Word and then listen to what the Spirit of God has to say back to you. We have left room for you to write down many of the revelations that God will give you, but you should keep a journal handy in case you need more room to write.

Get ready! This is exciting! You are about to change your life and many other lives, too! Go for it!

The Word works when you work the Word!

Day One

Ephesians 1:17-23

I pray that the God of our Lord Jesus Christ, the Father of glory, may grant __________ a spirit of wisdom and revelation [of insight into mysteries and secrets] in the [deep and intimate] knowledge of Him. By having the eyes of __________'s heart flooded with light, so that __________ can know and understand the hope to which He has called __________, and how rich is His glorious inheritance in the saints (His set-apart ones). And [so that __________ can know and understand] what is the immeasurable and unlimited and surpassing greatness of His power in and for __________, who believes, as demonstrated in the working of His mighty strength, which He exerted in Christ when He raised Him from the dead and seated Him at His [own] right hand in the heavenly [places], far above all rule and authority and power and dominion and every name that is named [above every title that can be conferred], not only in this age and in this world, but also in the age and the world which are to come. And He has put all things under His feet and has appointed Him the universal and supreme Head of the church [a headship exercised throughout the church], which is His body, the fullness of Him Who fills all in all [for in that body lives the full measure of Him Who makes everything complete, and Who fills everything everywhere with Himself].

I encourage you to pray one name at a time all the way through the scripture out loud.

After you have finished praying all the names on your prayer list, you can pray in your prayer language or just fellowship with God. Many times you will receive the interpretation of your prayers when you listen and are quiet. This is a great way to meditate on God's Word. Learn to listen, too! (Use the space provided to write down any thoughts you might want to remember. You can use your journal, too!)

Day Two

Ephesians 3:14-21

For this reason [seeing the greatness of this plan by which is built together in Christ], __________ bows his/her knees before the Father of our Lord Jesus Christ, for whom every family on earth and in heaven is named [that Father from Whom all fatherhood takes its title and derives its name].

May He grant __________ out of the rich treasury of His glory to be strengthened and reinforced with mighty power in the inner man by the [Holy] Spirit [Himself indwelling __________'s innermost being and personality]. May Christ through __________'s faith [actually] dwell (settle down, abide, make His permanent home) in __________'s heart! May __________ be rooted deep in love and founded securely on love, that __________ may have the power and be strong to apprehend and grasp with all the saints [God's devoted people, the experience of that love] what is the breadth and length and height and depth [of it]; [That __________ may really come] to know [practically, through experience for himself/herself] the love of Christ, which far surpasses mere knowledge [without experience]; that __________ may be filled [through all his/her being], unto all the fullness of God [may have the richest measure of the divine Presence, and become a body wholly filled and flooded with God Himself!]

Now to Him Who, by (in consequence of) the [action of His] power that is at work within __________ is able to [carry out His purpose and] do superabundantly, far over and above all that __________ dares ask or think [infinitely beyond __________'s highest prayers, desires, thoughts, hopes, or dreams].

To Him be glory in the church and in Christ Jesus throughout all generations forever and ever.

Amen (so be it).

For your prayer thoughts. Remember to meditate (be quiet and listen to God) and pray in your prayer language.

Day Three

John 8:32

And __________ will know the truth and the truth will set __________ free.

Luke 10:19

Jesus has given __________ authority and power to trample upon serpents and scorpions, and [physical and mental strength and ability] over all the power that the enemy (possesses) and nothing shall in any way harm __________.

John 3:16

For God so greatly loved and dearly prized the world that He [even] gave up His only begotten (unique) Son, so that __________, who believes in (trusts in, clings to, relies on) Him shall not

perish (come to destruction, or be lo
__________ has eternal (everlasting) life

Remember to pray and meditate.

A place for your prayer thoughts.

Day Four

Psalm 100

__________ will make a joyful noise to the Lord, yes, even all our lands! __________ will serve the Lord with gladness! __________ will come before His presence with singing! __________ will know (perceive, recognize, and understand with approval) that the Lord is God! It is He who has made __________ and not we ourselves (and __________ is His!).

__________ is His people and the sheep of His pasture.

__________ will enter into His gates with thanksgiving and a thank offering and into His courts with praise!

__________ will be thankful and say so to Him, __________ will bless and affectionately praise His name! For the Lord is good; His mercy and loving-kindness are everlasting, His faithfulness and truth endure to all generations.

Prayer changes things!

Day Five

Acts 26:18

I thank You, Lord, that You open __________'s eyes that __________ may turn from darkness to light and from the power of Satan to God, so that __________ may receive forgiveness and release from his/her sins and a place and portion among those who are consecrated and purified by faith in Christ.

God is saying to you, "If my people... will humble themselves and pray... I will hear their cry and I will answer them."

Pray and listen to God!

____

____

Day Six

2 Corinthians 5:20,21

I thank You, Lord, that ________ is Christ's ambassador, God making His appeal as it were through ________. ________ [as Christ's personal representative] begs you for Christ's sake to lay hold of the divine favor [now offered to everyone] and thank You, Lord, that ________ is reconciled to God. For ________'s sake God made Christ [virtually] to be sin Who knew no sin, so that in and through Him ________ might become [endued with, viewed as being in, and example of] the righteousness of God [what ________ ought to be, approved and acceptable and in right relationship with Christ, by Christ's goodness].

The Word works!

Day Six

Day Seven

Galatians 1:3-5

I thank You, Lord, that grace and spiritual blessing be to __________ and [soul] peace from God the Father and our Lord Jesus Christ (the Messiah) be __________'s. I thank You, Lord, that Christ gave (yielded) Himself up [to atone] for __________'s sins [and to save and sanctify __________], in order to rescue and deliver __________ from this present wicked age and world order, in accordance with the will and purpose and plan of our God and Father. To Christ [be ascribed all] the glory through all the ages of the ages and the eternities of the eternities! Amen (so be it).

Day Seven

Journal your thoughts.

Day Eight

Galatians 3:13, 14

Christ purchased __________'s freedom [redeeming __________] from the curse (doom) of the Law [and its condemnation] by [Himself] becoming a curse for __________, for it is written [in the Scriptures], Cursed is everyone who hangs on a tree (is crucified); To the end that through [__________'s receiving] Christ Jesus, the blessing [promised] to Abraham might come upon __________, so that __________ through faith might receive [the realization of] the promise of the [Holy] Spirit.

Use your journal! Write down what God is saying!

Day Nine

Psalm 103:1-6

__________ will bless (affectionately, gratefully praise) the Lord, O __________'s soul; and all that is (deepest) within __________, __________ will bless His holy name! __________ will bless (affectionately, gratefully praise) the Lord, O __________'s soul, and __________ will not forget (one of) all His benefits Who forgives (every one of) all __________'s iniquities, Who heals (each one of) all __________'s diseases, Who redeems __________'s life from the pit and corruption, Who beautifies, dignifies, and crowns __________ with loving-kindness and tender mercy; Who satisfies __________'s mouth (__________'s necessity and desire at his/her personal age and situation) with good so that __________'s youth, renewed, is like the eagle's [strong, overcoming, and soaring]! The Lord executes righteousness and justice (not for __________ only, but) for all who are oppressed.

Prayer Thoughts...

____

____

____

____

____

____

____

____

____

____

Day Ten

Psalm 91:1-10

__________, who dwell(s) in the secret place of the Most High shall remain stable and fixed under the shadow of the Almighty [Whose power no foe can withstand]. __________ will say of the Lord, "You are my Refuge and my Fortress, my God; on You I lean and rely, and in You I [confidently] trust!" For [then] the Lord will deliver __________ from the snare of the fowler and from the deadly pestilence. [Then] He will cover __________ with His pinions, and under His wings shall __________ trust and find refuge; His truth and His faithfulness are a shield and a buckler. __________ shall not be afraid of the terror of the night, nor of the arrow (the evil plots and slanders of the wicked) that flies by day, nor of the pestilence that stalks in darkness, nor of the destruction and sudden death that surprise and lay waste at noonday. A thousand may fall at __________'s side, and ten thousand at his/her right hand, but it shall not come near him/her. Only a spectator shall __________ be, [himself/herself inaccessible in the secret place of the Most High] as __________ witnesses the reward of the wicked. Because __________ has made the Lord his/her refuge, and the Most High his/her dwelling place, there shall no evil befall __________ nor any plague or calamity come near __________'s tent.

Pray in the Spirit! God will talk to you.

____

____

____

____

Day Eleven

Psalm 91:11-16

For He will give His angels [especial] charge over __________ to accompany and defend and preserve __________ in all his/her ways [of obedience and service]. They shall bear __________ up on their hands, lest __________ dashes his/her foot against a stone. __________ shall tread upon the lion and adder: the young lion and the serpent shall __________ trample underfoot. Because __________ has set his/her love upon the Lord, therefore the Lord will deliver __________; the Lord will set __________ on high, because he/she knows and understands the Lord's Name [has a personal knowledge of the Lord's mercy, love, and kindness—trusts and relies on the Lord, knowing that the Lord will never forsake ________, no, never]. ________ shall call upon the Lord, and the Lord will answer him/her; The Lord will be with ________ in trouble, the Lord will deliver ________ and honor him/her. With long life the Lord will satisfy ________ and show him/her the Lord's salvation.

The Word works when you work the Word!

____

____

____

____

____

____

____

____

____

Day Twelve

Matthew 21:21,22

I thank You, Lord, that __________ has faith (a firm relying trust) and does not doubt. I thank You, Father God, that You will not only do what has been done to the fig tree when it was cursed and it withered and died, but even if __________ says to this mountain, "Be taken up and cast into the sea, it will be done." And whatever __________ asks for in prayer, having faith and [really] believing, __________ will receive, in Jesus name. Amen (so be it.)

____

____

____

Day Thirteen

Matthew 22:37-39

__________ will love the Lord his/her God with all his/her heart and with all his/her soul and with all his/her mind (intellect). This is the great (most important, principal) and first commandment. And the second is like it: __________ will love his/her neighbor as he/she does himself/herself in Jesus' name. Amen (so be it.)

____

____

____

____

____

____

Day Fourteen

Luke 4:18, 19

The Spirit of the Lord is upon __________ because the Father God has anointed __________ to preach the good news (the Gospel) to the poor; He has sent __________ to announce release to the captives and recovery of sight to the blind, to send forth as delivered those who are oppressed [who are downtrodden, bruised, crushed, and broken down by calamity], to proclaim the accepted and acceptable year of the Lord [the day when salvation and the free favors of God profusely abound.]

____

____

Day Fifteen

Mark 16:15-18

And Jesus said to __________,"Go into all the world and preach and publish openly the good news (the Gospel) to every creature [of the whole human race]. __________ who believes (who adheres to and trusts in and relies on the Gospel and Jesus Who it sets forth] and is baptized will be saved (from the penalty of eternal death); But he who does not believe [who does not adhere to and trust in and rely on the Gospel and Jesus Whom it sets forth] will be condemned. And these attesting signs will accompany __________ who believes: in Jesus' name __________ will drive out demons; __________ will speak in new languages; __________ will pick up serpents; and [even] if ________ drinks anything deadly, it will not hurt ________; ________ will lay his/her hands on the sick, and the sick will get well, in Jesus' mighty and miraculous name. Amen, (so be it.)

Day Sixteen

Jeremiah 29: 11-14

For I know the thoughts and plans that I have for __________ says the Lord, thoughts and plans for welfare and peace and not for evil, to give __________ hope in his/her final outcome. Then __________ will call upon Me, and __________ will come and pray to Me, and I, the Lord, will hear and heed __________. Then __________ will seek Me, inquire for, and require Me (as a vital necessity) and find Me, the Lord, when __________ searches for Me with all his/her heart. I will be found by __________ says the Lord, and I will release __________ from captivity and gather __________ from all the nations and all the places to which I have driven __________, says the Lord, and I will bring ________ back to the place from which I caused ________ to be carried away captive.

Day Seventeen

Isaiah 43:18, 19

__________ will not (earnestly) remember the former things; neither consider the things of old. Behold, the Lord is doing a new thing for __________! Now it springs forth: __________ will perceive it and know it and will give heed to it! God will even make a way in the wilderness and rivers in the desert for __________ in Jesus' name. Amen, (so be it).

Isaiah 44:3

For the Lord will pour water upon __________ who is thirsty, and floods upon the dry ground. The Lord will pour His Spirit upon __________'s offspring, and the Lord's blessing upon __________'s descendants. And they shall spring up among the grass like willows or poplars by the watercourses, in Jesus' name. Amen, (so be it).

Day Eighteen

Isaiah 51:16

The Lord has put His Words in __________'s mouth and has covered __________ with the shadow of His hand.

Philippians 1:9-11

And this I pray: that __________'s love may abound yet more and more and extend to its fullest development in knowledge and all keen insight [that __________'s love may display itself in greater depth of acquaintance and more comprehensive discernment], so that __________ may surely learn to sense what is vital, and approve and prize what is excellent and of real value [recognizing the highest and the best, and distinguishing the moral differences], and that __________ may be untainted and pure and unerring and blameless [so that with a heart sincere and certain and unsullied, __________ may approach] the day of Christ [not stumbling nor causing others to stumble]. May __________ abound in and be filled with the fruits of righteousness (of right standing with God and right doing) which come through Jesus Christ (the Anointed One), to the honor and praise of God [that His glory may be both manifested and recognized].

Day Nineteen

1 Peter 2:9-12

__________ is a chosen race, a royal priesthood, a dedicated nation, [God's] own purchased special person, that __________ may set forth the wonderful deeds and display the virtues and perfections of Him Who called __________ out of darkness into His marvelous light. Once __________ was not a people at all, but now is God's person; once __________ was unpitied, but now __________ is pitied and has received mercy. __________ will abstain from the sensual urges (the evil desires, the passions of the flesh, his/her lower nature) that wage war against his/her soul. __________ will conduct himself/herself properly (honorably, righteously) among his/her peers, so that, although they may slander __________ as an evildoer, [yet] they may be witnessing __________'s good deeds [come to] glorify God in the day of inspection [when God shall look upon __________ as a pastor or shepherd looks over his flock] in Jesus' name. Amen, (so be it.)

Day Twenty

1 Peter 3:12

For the eyes of the Lord are upon __________(who is upright and in right standing with God), and His ears are attentive to __________'s prayer. But the face of the Lord is against those who practice evil [to oppose __________ to frustrate, and defeat __________] in Jesus' name. Amen, (so be it).

Philippians 4:13

________ has strength for all things in Christ Who empowers him/her. [__________ is ready for anything and equal to anything through Him Who infuses inner strength into __________; __________ is self sufficient in Christ's sufficiency].

Day Twenty

Proverbs 18:16

__________'s gift makes room for him/her and brings him/her before great men.

Day Twenty-one

Philippians 4:6-9, 11

__________ will not fret or have any anxiety about anything, but in every circumstance and in everything, by prayer and petition (definite requests), with thanksgiving, __________ will make his/her wants known to God. And God's peace [shall be__________'s, that tranquil state of a soul assured of its salvation through Christ, and so fearing nothing from God and being content with its earthly lot of whatever sort that is, that peace] which transcends all understanding shall garrison and mount guard over __________'s heart and mind in Christ Jesus. Whatever is true, whatever is worthy of reverence and is honorable and seemly, whatever is just, whatever is pure, whatever is lovely and lovable, whatever is kind and winsome and gracious, if there is any virtue and excellence, if there is anything worthy of praise, __________ will think on and weigh and take account of these things [fix his/her mind on them]. __________ will practice what he/she has learned and received and heard and seen and __________ will model his/her way of living on it, and the God of peace (of untroubled, undisturbed well-being) will be with __________. __________ has learned how to be content (satisfied to the point where he/she is not disturbed or disquieted) in whatever state that he/she is in, in the mighty name of Jesus. Amen, (so be it).

Journal and Pray!

____

____

____

____

Day Twenty-two

Colossians 1:9-14

For this reason we also from the day we heard of it, have not ceased to pray and make [special] request for __________, [asking] that __________ may be filled with the full (deep and clear) knowledge of Christ's will in all spiritual wisdom [in comprehensive insight into the ways and purposes of God] and in understanding and discernment of spiritual things—that __________ may walk (live and conduct himself/herself) in a manner worthy of the Lord, fully pleasing to Him and desiring to please Him in all things, bearing fruit in every good work and steadily growing and increasing in and by the knowledge of God [with fuller, deeper, and clearer insight, acquaintance, and recognition]. [We pray] that ________ may be invigorated and strengthened with all power according to the might of Christ's glory, [to exercise] every kind of endurance and patience (perseverance and forbearance) with joy, giving thanks to the Father, Who has qualified and made ________ fit to share the portion which is the inheritance of the saints (God's holy people) in the Light. [The Father] has delivered and drawn ________ to Himself out of the control and the dominion of darkness and has transferred ________ into the Kingdom of the Son of His love, in whom we have our redemption through Christ's blood, [which means] the forgiveness of ________'s sins.

Pray in the Spirit!

Day Twenty-three

Proverbs 16:3

__________ rolls his/her works upon the Lord [__________ commits and trusts them wholly to Him; He will cause __________'s thoughts to become agreeable to His will, and] so shall __________'s plans be established and succeed in Jesus' name. Amen, (so be it).

Proverbs 15:30

The light in the eyes [of __________ whose heart is joyful] rejoices the hearts of others, and good news nourishes __________'s bones in Jesus' name. Amen, (so be it).

Write down your thoughts.

____

____

Day Twenty-four

Proverbs 15:15b

__________ has a glad heart, and because he/she has a glad heart __________ has a continual feast (regardless of circumstances).

Proverbs 15:4

__________ has a gentle tongue which brings with it healing power and is a tree of life to those who hear it in Jesus' name. Amen, (so be it).

Remember, the Word works!

____

____

____

Day Twenty-five

Psalm 1:1-3

Blessed (happy, fortunate, prosperous, and enviable) is ___________ who walks and lives not in the counsel of the ungodly [following their advice, their plans and purposes], nor does ___________ stand [submissive and inactive] in the path where sinners walk, nor does ___________ sit down [to relax and rest] where the scornful [and the mockers] gather. But ___________'s delight and desire is in the law of the Lord, and on His law [the precepts, the instructions, the teachings of God] does ___________ habitually meditate (ponder and study) by day and by night. And ___________ shall be like a tree firmly planted [and tended] by the streams of water, ready to bring forth its fruit in its season; its leaf also shall not fade or wither; and everything ___________ does shall prosper [and come to maturity].

Day Twenty-six

Psalm 6:10

Let all __________'s enemies be ashamed and sorely troubled; let them turn back and be put to shame suddenly.

Isaiah 1:19

__________ is willing and obedient and he/she shall eat the good of the land in Jesus' name. Amen, (so be it).

____

____

____

____

____

Day Twenty-seven

Isaiah 54:17

But no weapon that is formed against ________ shall prosper, and every tongue that shall rise against ________ in judgment he/she shall show to be in the wrong. This [peace, righteousness, security, triumph over opposition] is the heritage of ________, the servant of the Lord [in whom the ideal Servant of the Lord is reproduced]; this is the righteousness or the vindication which he/she obtains from the Lord [this is that which the Lord imparts to ________ as his/her justification], in Jesus' name. Amen, (so be it).

Use your journal to write down your thoughts.

Day Twenty-eight

Isaiah 55:2b,3,6

__________ will hearken diligently to the Lord, and __________ will eat what is good, and he/she will let his/her soul delight itself in fatness [the profuseness of spiritual joy].

__________ will incline his/her ear [submitting and consenting to the divine will] and __________ will come to the Lord; he/she will hear, and his/her soul will revive; and the Lord will make an everlasting covenant or league with __________, even the sure mercy (kindness, goodwill, and compassion) promised to David will be his/hers. __________ will seek, inquire for, and require the Lord while He may be found [claiming the Lord by necessity and by right];

Day Twenty-eight

__________ will call upon the Lord while He is near.

Day Twenty-nine

Isaiah 55:8-13

The Lord says, "__________, My thoughts are not your thoughts neither are your ways My ways. For as the heavens are higher than the earth, so are My ways higher than your ways and My thoughts higher than your thoughts. For as the rain and snow come down from the heavens, and return not there again, but water the earth and make it bring forth and sprout, that it may give seed to the sower and bread to the eater, so shall My Word be that goes forth out of My mouth: it shall not return to Me void (without producing any effect, useless), but it shall accomplish that which I please and purpose, and it shall prosper in the thing for which I sent it. For you,

__________, shall go out[from the spiritual exile caused by sin and evil into the holyland] with joy and be led forth [by your Leader, the Lord Himself, and His Word] with peace; the mountains and the hills shall break forth before you, __________, into singing, and all the trees of the field shall clap their hands. Instead of the thorn shall come up the cypress tree, and instead of the brier shall come up the myrtle tree; and it shall be to the Lord for a name of renown, for an everlasting sign [of jubilant exaltation] and memorial [to His praise], which shall not be cut off to you, __________, in the name of Jesus. Amen, (so be it)."

Prayer Journal

____

____

____

____

____

Day Thirty

Isaiah 59:21

This is a word from the Lord to you, __________. __________, as for Me, this is My covenant or league with you: My Spirit, Who is upon you, [and Who writes the law of God inwardly on the heart], and My words which I have put in your mouth, __________ shall not depart out of your mouth, or out of the mouths of your [true, spiritual] children, or out of the mouths of your children's children, says the Lord, to you, from henceforth and forever in Jesus' name. Amen, (so be it).

Get out your journal and write as He speaks.

Day Thirty-one

Psalm 145:9

The Lord is good to __________, and His tender mercies are over all His works [the entirety of things created].

Proverbs 12:1a-2a

__________ loves instruction and correction (and) loves knowledge. __________ is a good man/woman and obtains favor from the Lord.

Pray and expect a miracle for your family!

Day Thirty-two

Isaiah 60:1-5

__________ shall arise [from the depression and the prostration in which circumstances have kept him/her. __________ shall rise to a new life]! __________ shall shine [be radiant with the glory of the Lord], for __________'s light has come, and the glory of the Lord has risen upon __________. For behold, darkness shall cover the earth, and dense darkness [all] peoples, but the Lord shall arise upon __________, and His glory shall be seen on __________, and nations shall come to __________'s light, and kings to the brightness of __________'s rising. __________ will lift up his/her eyes round about him/her and see! They all gather them-

selves together, they come to ________.
________'s sons shall come from afar, and his/her daughters shall be carried and nursed in the arms. Then ________ shall see and be radiant, and his/her heart shall thrill and tremble with joy [at the glorious deliverance] and be enlarged; because the abundant wealth of the [Dead] Sea shall be turned to ________, unto ________ shall the nations come with their treasures in Jesus' name. Amen (so be it).

Don't forget to pray in the Spirit!

____

____

____

____

____

____

____

____

Day Thirty-three

Isaiah 61:1-3, 10, 11

The Spirit of the Lord God is upon __________, because the Lord has anointed and qualified __________ to preach the Gospel of good tidings to the meek, the poor, and afflicted; He has sent __________ to bind up and heal the brokenhearted, to proclaim liberty to the [physical and spiritual] captives and the opening of the prison and of the eyes to those who are bound, to proclaim the acceptable year of the Lord [the year of His favor] and the day of vengeance of our God, to comfort all who mourn, to grant [consolation and joy] to those who mourn in Zion — to give them an ornament (a garland or diadem) of beauty instead of ashes, the oil of joy instead of mourning, the garment [expressive] of praise instead of a heavy, burdened, and failing spirit — that they may be called oaks of righteousness [lofty, strong, and magnificent, distinguished for uprightness, justice, and right standing with God], the planting of the Lord, that He may be glorified. __________ will greatly rejoice in the Lord, his/her soul will exult in our God; for He has clothed __________ with the garments of salvation, He has covered __________ with the robes of righteousness, as a bridegroom decks himself with a garland, and as a bride adorns herself with her jewels. For as [surely as] the earth brings forth its shoots, and as a garden causes what is sown in it to bring forth, so [surely] the Lord God will cause rightness and justice and praise to spring forth before all the nations [through the self-fulfilling power of His word] in __________'s life in Jesus' name. Amen, (so be it). *Use your journal...*

Day Thirty-four

Psalm 18:1-6, 16

__________ loves the Lord fervently and devotedly, O Lord, his/her strength. The Lord is __________'s Rock, his/her Fortress, and his/her Deliverer; his/her God, his/her keen and firm Strength in whom __________ will trust and take refuge, his/her Shield, and the Horn of his/her salvation, his/her High Tower. __________ will call upon the Lord, Who is to be praised; so shall __________ be saved from his/her enemies. The cords or bands of death surrounded __________, and the streams of ungodliness and the torrents of ruin terrified him/her. The cords of Sheol (the place of the dead) surrounded him/her; the snares of death confronted and came upon him/her. In his/her distress [when seemingly closed in] __________ called upon the Lord and cried to God: He heard his/her voice out of His temple (heavenly dwelling place), and his/her cry came before Him, into His [very] ears. He reached from on high, He took __________; He drew him/her out of many waters.

Miracles are coming! Keep praying...

Day Thirty-five

Psalm 18:17,28,29,30,33,34,35

He delivered __________ from his/her strong enemy and from those who hated and abhorred __________, for they were too strong for him/her. For You cause __________'s lamp to be lighted and to shine; the Lord our God illumines his/her darkness. For by You, Lord, __________ can run through a troop, and by our God __________ can leap over a wall. As for God, His way is perfect! The word of the Lord is tested and tried; He is a shield to __________ who takes refuge and puts his/her trust in Him. He makes __________'s feet like hinds' feet [able to stand firmly or make progress on the dangerous heights of testing and trouble];

Day Thirty-five

He sets __________ securely upon his/her high places. He teaches __________'s hands to war, so that his/her arms can bend a bow of bronze. God has given __________ the shield of His salvation, and the Father God's right hand has held __________ up; God's gentleness and condescension have made __________ great in Jesus' name. Amen, (so be it).

Day Thirty-six

Psalm 18:36-45

You, Father God, have given plenty of room for __________'s steps under him/her, that his/her feet would not slip. __________ pursued his/her enemies and overtook them; neither did __________ turn again till they were consumed. __________ smote them so that they were not able to rise; they fell wounded under his/her feet. For You, Lord, have girded __________ with strength for the battle; You have subdued under him/her and caused to bow down those who rose up against him/her. You, Lord, have also made __________'s enemies turn their backs to him/her, that he/she might cut off those who hate him/her. They cried [for help], but there was none to deliver even unto the Lord, but You, Lord, answered them not. Then __________ beat them small as the dust before the wind; __________ emptied them out as the dirt and mire of the streets. You, Lord, have delivered __________ from the strivings of the people; You made him/her the head of nations; a people he/she had not known served him/her. As soon as they heard of __________, they obeyed him/her; foreigners submitted themselves cringingly and yielded feigned obedience to him/her. Foreigners lost heart and came trembling out of their caves or strongholds.

(This could be demonic strongholds and places of hiding. Foreigners are those who are not in the family or under the family covering. For example: demons are foreigners to God. They are not like God. They are different, foreign to Him, so think on that as you pray this prayer.)

Use your journal!

Day Thirty-seven

Psalm 18:46-50

The Lord lives! Blessed be __________'s Rock; and let the God of __________'s salvation be exalted. The God Who avenges __________ and subdues peoples under him/her, Who delivers __________ from his/her enemies; yes, You, Lord, lift __________ up above those who rise up against him/her; You deliver him/her from the man of violence. Therefore will __________ give thanks and extol You, Lord, among the nations, and sing praises to Your Name. Great deliverances and triumphs gives He to His king; and He shows mercy and steadfast love to his anointed, and to his/her offspring forever, in the mighty name of Jesus. Amen (so be it)!

(Remember when praying this type of warfare prayer, the enemy can be a natural man or a supernatural demonic force that has been sent against God's people. Don't concern yourself with the enemy. God will take care of you. Focus on God when you pray!)

Day Thirty-eight

Matthew 10:31,32

__________ will not fear, for __________ is of more value than many sparrows to the Lord. Therefore, __________ acknowledges Jesus before men and confesses Jesus [out of a state of oneness with Jesus]. Jesus will also acknowledge __________ before the Father God Who is in heaven and __________ will confess [that Jesus is abiding in] him/her, in Jesus' name. Amen, (so be it).

___

___

___

___

___

Day Thirty-nine

Matthew 16:19

I thank You, Lord, that You give to __________ the keys of the kingdom of heaven; and whatever __________ binds (declares to be improper and unlawful) on earth must be what is already bound in heaven; and whatever __________ looses (declares lawful) on earth must be what is already loosed in heaven in Jesus' mighty name. Amen, (so be it).

(Remember, the above Scriptures tell us that God has given to us two keys to the kingdom of heaven. They are: #1 binding, #2 loosing.)

____

____

____

Day Forty

Matthew 18:18-20

I thank You, Lord, that whatever __________ forbids and declares to be improper and unlawful on earth must be what is already forbidden in heaven, and whatever __________ permits and declares proper and lawful on earth must be what is already permitted in heaven. I thank You, Lord, that when __________ and anyone else on the earth agree (harmonize together, making a symphony together) about whatever [anything and everything] that they may ask, it will come to pass and be done for them by My Father in heaven. I thank You, Lord, that wherever two or three are gathered together in Your name, there You are in the midst of them.

I like to end these past two days of praying with this prayer:

I thank You, Lord, that I declare the following to be improper and unlawful on earth concerning my family, friends, staff, and ministry partners: poverty, sickness, disease, plague, dishonest speech, fleshly talk, unrighteousness, doubt, unbelief, demonic captivity, suicide, anorexia, bulimia, overeating, depression, oppression, rebellion, any attack from demonic forces of any kind, turmoil, strife, ungodly thoughts and actions, abuse, (and any others you may think of). All these are already unlawful and improper in heaven; therefore, we have a right and we take our rightful authority to declare all of these things listed to be bound, inoperative, and ineffective. These things are not permitted. They are not lawful on this earth concerning our family, friends, staff, and ministry family.

I thank You, Lord, that I declare the following to be proper and lawful on this earth in our family, friends, staff, and ministry family, by our rightful God-given authority. Prosperity is proper and lawful. It is loosed over us. Health, healing, freedom, peace, tranquility, protection from all human, inhuman, and demonic enemies, submissiveness, obedience, faith, hope, love, godly speech, godly mouths and tongues, godly thoughts and actions are all loosed over us. These are all activated, effective, operational, and loosed in our lives today in Jesus' name. Amen, (so be it).

Now remember to pray in your prayer language, the Holy Spirit of God, each day.

Conclusion

Since you have finished praying all 40 days, now start over tomorrow and pray these 40 days of scripture prayers again! Add to your prayer list as you feel led of the Holy Spirit to do so. As you discipline yourself to spend this time each day in prayer for yourself and others, I know that you will begin to see, feel, and know a change in yourself and in others. You are filling yourself with God's Word, and you are also putting it into the atmosphere by speaking it to the Father God in prayer. He really does watch over His Word to perform it, and you are allowing that to happen by your obedience to pray. This really makes the devil mad because he doesn't want you to take your God-given, rightful authority in the spirit realm—so do it again!

The effectual fervent prayer of a righteous man (male and female) avails much, so get with it! Let's get to availing much in our lives through righteous prayer to our heavenly Father God.

Pray, friends, pray! Remember, you may be the only one who will be obedient to pray for certain ones. Do it. Don't put it off or expect someone else to do it. It's your calling. Speak the Word of God out of your mouth and watch God perform His Word. He will do His part, never worry! It's rightfully ours, so take it!

If we don't partake of the work of Christ on the cross, we are saying that what He did was in vain. No! What Christ did was not in vain! Receive today!

The Word works when you work the Word!

Prayer of Salvation

God loves you—no matter who you are, no matter what your past. God loves you so much that He gave His one and only begotten Son for you. The Bible tells us that "...whoever believes in him shall not perish but have eternal life" (John 3:16 NIV). Jesus laid down His life and rose again so that we could spend eternity with Him in heaven and experience His absolute best on earth. If you would like to receive Jesus into your life, say the following prayer out loud and mean it from your heart.

Heavenly Father, I come to You admitting that I am a sinner. Right now, I choose to turn away from sin, and I ask You to cleanse me of all unrighteousness. I believe that Your Son, Jesus, died on the cross to take away my sins. I also believe that He rose again from the dead so that I might be forgiven of my sins and made righteous through faith in Him. I call upon the name of Jesus Christ to be the Lord and Savior of my life. Jesus, I choose to follow You and ask that You fill me with the power of the Holy Spirit. I declare right now that I am a child of God. I am free from sin and full of the righteousness of God. I am saved in Jesus' name. Amen.

Contact us to let us know you prayed this prayer!

Salem Family Ministries
P.O. Box 701287
Tulsa, Oklahoma 74170

Please include your prayer requests and comments when you write.

About the Authors

Harry and Cheryl Salem have a beautiful love story to tell. It began in 1985, when a confident, successful businessman met Miss America. Sparks flew and they soon wed, but the honeymoon didn't last forever. Through desperate, low valleys and tremendous high places, this couple has walked - not always in perfect harmony, but always together and in agreement. This bond was tested beyond imagination in 1999 as they walked through the darkest valley of all.

Their daughter, Gabrielle, was stricken with a terminal illness and the family was devastated. Throughout this journey, Harry and Cheryl never lost sight of their commitment to trusting God and walking in agreement, even as their precious little one graduated to Heaven in November 23, 1999. They were devastated, but not defeated.

Salem Family Ministries focuses on family and restoration. They also lead motivational meetings and men's and ladies' conferences on the subjects of overcoming obstacles such as abuse, abandonment, poor self-image and financial difficulty.

Harry and Cheryl have written over 25 books, including, *An Angel's Touch* (a top-25 best-seller), *Distractions from Destiny, From Grief to Glory* and their latest book on relationships, *2 Becoming 1*.

Harry and Cheryl have two sons, Harry III and Roman, and a beautiful daughter, Gabrielle, who lives in Heaven.

"Gabrielle is not in our past, but she is in our future"

Other Books by Harry & Cheryl Salem

2 Becoming 1
The Choice is Yours
40 Day Prayer Journal - Overcoming Fear
Every Body Needs Balance
From Grief to Glory
Distractions from Destiny
From Mourning to Morning
Speak the Word over Your Family for Finances
Speak the Word over Your Family for Healing
Covenant Conquerors - Book 3 (For Kids)
Warriors of the Word/Fight in the Heavenlies - Books 1 & 2 (For Kids)
Fight in the Heavenlies (out of print)
It's Too Soon to Give Up
Being #1 at Being #2
For Men Only
An Angel's Touch
A Royal Child
The Mommy Book
Simple Facts about Salvation, Healing & the Holy Ghost (out of print)
Health & Beauty Secrets (out of print)
Choose to be Happy (out of print)
Abuse...Bruised but Not Broken
You Are Somebody
A Bright Shining Place - The Story of a Miracle

The Salems are in demand as
conference, church,
and crusade speakers. . .

For booking information
or a more complete
listing of all ministry items,
please contact us at:

Salem Family Ministries
P.O. Box 701287 Tulsa, OK 74170
(918)369-8008 Fax 369-8004
www.salemfamilyministries.org

Check out these and other titles by

Harry & Cheryl Salem!